Wildwood Christian Fellowship.

Living Tr

CW01669506

Loving t

Understanding the New Testament
with the LIVING BIBLE

To Audrey and John
wishing you God's blessing
from David Taylor.

Loving the Jesus Way

Author: David L. Taylor
Artist: John Pickering

Scripture Union 47 Marylebone Lane London W1M 6AX

Scripture Union 1978
First published 1978
ISBN 0 85421 613 8

Printed in England by Hazell Watson & Viney Ltd, Aylesbury, Bucks

Introducing you . . .

'Why don't you publish something for older teens and adults that is easy to use, attractive to look at and covers the basic teaching of the Bible?'

That's the sort of request that came to me through letters and conversations —and in response here is the LIVING TRUTH series!

I hope the combination of Bible readings, comments and prayers are right for you. I think you'll agree that the cartoons hit home the truth in a humorous yet positive way.

The editor

From the editor

I first got in touch with David Taylor (ex teacher) when he entered a competition for writers run by Scripture Union. He's the minister of Rising Brook Baptist Church in Stafford.

The Taylor family: Children from left to right: Helen, Pauline, John with their parents: Kathleen and David.

As you can see from the photograph, he's a family man with a wife and three children. The whole family go swimming together, and David enjoys a game of squash. When he came into my office recently he had a badly bruised nose—not because of an interest in boxing, but because he sometimes joins in a game of football with the boys!

John Pickering says that after nine years in graphics, handling advertising and packaging accounts for some of Britain's leading stores, working as an art editor for an American magazine and designing and illustrating various promotional materials, he decided to become a free-lance artist/designer. He felt that there ought to be more creative ways to use his life for God than advertising foundation garments or shoes!

John and his wife, Fran, live in the beautiful English countryside. His studio looks out over tree-bordered fields sloping to a gentle horizon—a scene to inspire creativity for God.

1
Are you a drifter?

Before anything else existed, there was Christ with God. He has always been alive and is himself God. He created everything there is—nothing exists that he didn't make. Eternal life is in him, and this life gives light to all mankind.

John chapter 1, verses 1-4

Do you feel that you are a victim of circumstances, or that the course of your life is out of your hands? Do you question whether there is any real purpose in life? If you think in this way, it is helpful to look back to the beginning of the world to discover God's purpose in creation.

It is only as you read the Bible that you understand that *all* life has its beginning in Jesus Christ. The Gospel of John does not contain any record of Jesus' birth, but John makes it clear that the Jesus he knew was no ordinary man. As God and Creator He alone can give meaning and direction to life. John introduces you to God's answer to all your needs. Faith in Christ will help you to discover the true meaning of your life—a life that begins in Christ and has no ending.

Thank God that through Jesus Christ you can find the true meaning of life. Praise Him for His creation.

WHAT'S IN A

Mr and Mrs X never referred to their unborn child as 'it'. Instead they agreed about the possible names and spoke of 'Paul Mary'! After his safe arrival they simply dropped the 'Mary'! If you met a couple who said that they were not giving their baby a name, rather they would speak of her as 22093X, how would you react? No one wants to be reduced to a mere number: names are personal and can be very appropriate.

When the angel announced to Joseph that Mary was going to have a son, he also gave the name—'Jesus' meaning 'Saviour'—one who would save His people from their sins. A great debate surrounded Jesus throughout His earthly life: Should He be called the *Messiah* (Christ)? Was this village carpenter from Nazareth the great promised deliverer for whom the Jews were eagerly waiting?

Some of His countrymen would only describe Jesus as a *prophet*—a man with an inspired message, or teacher—a clever person with interesting ideas. They refused to accept the one title which adequately describes Him—*the Son of God.* When we meet with Jesus our encounter is not just with another ordinary human being; we are being brought face to face with God.

Several million people are called by the name most popular in English-speaking countries—'*John*'. It means, 'The Lord is gracious.' John the apostle, who wrote both a Gospel and three letters, had discovered that God's grace was needed to change completely the nature of people like himself. Jesus had once given him the nickname 'son of thunder'. Now he writes with feeling about love and how Christians must be gracious and loving.

Mark—meaning 'war-like'—wrote Peter's memoirs, the Gospel of Mark. He picked up the nickname, 'stumpy fingers'. Originally *Peter* was known as Simon, but Jesus gave him the name Peter—the rock. For several years Peter did not live up to his name, being impetuous and unreliable. Later his early failures helped him to understand the pressures Christians have to face. He writes encouraging those going the Jesus way to stand firm in their faith.

2
Born into a new family

But although he made the world, the world didn't recognize him when he came. Even in his own land and among his own people, the Jews, he was not accepted. Only a few would welcome and receive him.

But to all who received him, he gave the right to become children of God. All they needed to do was to trust him to save them. All those who believe this are reborn—not a physical rebirth resulting from human passion or plan, but from the will of God.

John chapter 1, verses 10-13

'If Jesus were here today and did a miracle, then I'd believe in Him.' The person who talks in this way forgets that many of Jesus' contemporaries witnessed miracles . . . yet still refused to believe in Him. Even His own family, at this time, rejected His claims. But the true family of Jesus is the biggest miracle of all time.

If you recognize Jesus as the unique Son of God and commit your life to Him, then you are born into His family. Every time such a birth takes place it is a miracle planned by God to give His children the right to call Him 'Father'. You enter into a special relationship with Him.

I thank You, Lord, that as Your child I can call You 'Father'. I pray for all those in Your family. Please strengthen us and teach us to live lives that honour You.

3
Look at Jesus

And Christ took our human nature and lived here on earth among us and was full of loving forgiveness and truth. And some of us have seen his glory—the glory of the only Son of the heavenly Father.

John pointed him out to the people, telling the crowds, 'This is the one I was talking about when I said, "Someone is coming who is greater by far than I am—for he existed long before I did." '

We have all benefited from the rich blessings he brought to us . . . For Moses gave us only the Law with its rigid demands and merciless justice, while Jesus Christ brought us loving forgiveness as well.

No one has ever actually seen God, but, of course, his only Son has, for he is the companion of the Father and has told us all about him.

John chapter 1, verses 14-18

Have you ever asked, 'What's God like?' John gives the answer to this question. Look at Jesus—not a brief glance, but a steady concentration. As you keep your eyes on Him, you will discover more and more of what God is like.

But how can we look at Jesus? By giving time to read and think about what the Bible says about Him. By mixing with those who love Him and allow Him to control their lives. By talking to Him in prayer.

4

One who really matters

The next day John saw Jesus coming towards him and said, 'Look! There is the Lamb of God who takes away the world's sin! He is the one I was talking about when I said, "Soon a man far greater than I am is coming, who existed long before me." I didn't know he was the one, but I am here baptizing with water in order to point him out to the nation of Israel.'

John chapter 1, verses 29-31

Many people are willing to go to listen to great preachers. But if they are doing their job properly, these servants of God are preparing the way for Jesus. They point Him out to people as the Person who really matters. When we are in need, help may come to us from many directions and in various ways, but *only* Jesus can take away the sin that comes between us and God.

In Old Testament times when a Jew sinned he would take a lamb (or some other animal allowed in the law), and lay his hands on the animal's head before it was killed on the altar. In this way his sin was forgiven and he was accepted by God.

John the Baptist said that Jesus was like that lamb. He had come to take away the sin of the world, and He did that by dying on the cross at Calvary. The fact that God raised Him from the dead proves that His Son's sacrifice was accepted.

Ask God to help you to understand the sacrifice of the Lamb of God.

5

Getting to know Jesus

Then John described how he had seen the Holy Spirit in the form of a dove descending from heaven and resting upon Jesus. 'I didn't know he was the one,' John said again, 'but at the time God sent me to baptize he told me, "When you see the Holy Spirit descending and resting upon someone—he is the one you are looking for. He is the one who baptizes with the Holy Spirit." I saw it happen to this man, and I therefore testify that he is the Son of God.'

John chapter 1, verses 32-34

We can know about Jesus without realizing who He is and what He came to do. John the Baptist and Jesus were relatives who, as boys, probably played together, but until God gave him a special sign, John didn't realize that his cousin was the Messiah. Then John's eyes were opened to the truth: 'Jesus is the ONE—the great Saviour we are looking for. He's not a superman, He's the Son of God!' is John's stupendous conclusion.

Do you have any doubts about Jesus? Do you find it hard to believe what you've read in the past few pages? John was being extra careful and he was convinced. If there had been any questions left, he wouldn't have spoken as he did. He was sure and we can be just as sure.

Sometimes, Father, I find it hard to accept what the Bible tells me about Jesus. Please help me to believe what I read and to follow Him.

GUIDELINES for PRAYER

Guidelines for prayer are always a help and most of the numbered sections include a prayer or prayer idea. If not, look up the reference to a prayer page, and there you will find a relevant prayer to link up with the section you are reading. Take hold of the main idea and turn it into *your* prayer by adding your own thoughts and feelings, mentioning incidents from *your* life.

Jesus, who spent a lot of time praying, has much to teach you in the school of prayer. Major decisions, joys, problems, other people's needs—all led Him to prayer.

Although you can talk to God anywhere and at any time, get into the habit of having regular times for prayer. Try not to be in a hurry—read some of God's Word before you speak to Him. As you progress try writing your own prayers. The main themes to include are:

- worship—thanking God for His love;
- confession—saying sorry for your sin;
- prayer for others;
- prayer about personal needs and problems.

Prayer pages can be used as meditations, allowing you to think about some of the basic truths of the Christian faith. *Prayer page one* invites you to face up to the realities of life.

The theme of *prayer page two* is commitment to God. He supplies the necessary help and strength to live the Christian life.

Being a Christian isn't just doing certain religious activities, and on *prayer page three* you will see how your faith must be worked out in your day-to-day activities. Through prayer you will receive the power of God.

Christianity is different from all other religions because it shows us God seeking men and women rather than them trying to find their way to God. *Prayer page four* concentrates on Jesus the Saviour who has come to rescue us.

Witnessing to Jesus brings its own blessings and problems. On *prayer page five* you are encouraged to step out in faith, and tell others about Jesus.

On *prayer page six*, you see that God is in control, calling His people to trust Him at all times, even when there are many difficulties ahead.

6
The work you want

One day as Jesus was walking along the shores of the sea of Galilee, he saw Simon and his brother Andrew fishing with nets, for they were fishermen by trade.

Jesus called out to them, 'Come, follow me! And I will make you fishermen for men!' At once they left their nets and went with him.

A little farther up the beach, he saw Zebedee's sons, James and John, in a boat mending their nets. He called them, too, and immediately they left their father Zebedee in the boat with the hired men and went with him.

Mark chapter 1, verses 16-20

What do you look for in a new job?

- Pleasant conditions—a comfortable place and pleasant people to work with?
- Good money—enough for necessities and some luxuries?
- Job satisfaction—where you and your work matter to the management?

What did the disciples leave?

- Steady jobs with a regular income.
- The company of family and friends.
- The prestige of being their own bosses.

What do you think they expected to get out of following Jesus?

You might like to use prayer [1] on page 20.

STATUS
THE BOSS
MONEY

1 PRAYER PAGE

Open to God

1 Listening to God's call

Is God calling me to a new kind of work for Him? It may involve changing employment or mean a new job in church life. Make a note of the various possibilities. Then, pray: 'Lord, I am listening to what You are saying to me.'

(6, page 18)

2 When challenged by evil

Keep me, Lord, from being too interested or obsessed by the evil in the world. Stop me from going to the other extreme, thinking everything is all right. Help me, with Jesus' power, to fight against evil—both in my own life and wherever else I find it.

(7, page 21)

3 Jesus loves everybody

Write down some names of people for whom you can pray: People at home/people you meet during the day/people you meet on Sundays/people you meet through your hobbies.

(11, page 25)

7
Authority

Jesus and his companions now arrived at the town of Capernaum and on Saturday morning went into ... the synagogue—where he preached.

The congregation was surprised at his sermon because he spoke as an authority, and didn't try to prove his points by quoting others—quite unlike what they were used to hearing.

A man possessed by a demon was present and began shouting, ... 'I know who you are—the holy Son of God!'

Jesus curtly commanded the demon to say no more and to come out of the man. At that the evil spirit screamed and convulsed the man violently and left him. Amazement gripped the audience and they began discussing what had happened. 'What sort of new religion is this?' they asked excitedly. 'Why, even evil spirits obey his orders!'

Mark chapter 1, verses 21-27

'Who says so?' 'Why shouldn't I when everybody else does?' Authority is a subject always guaranteed to provoke lively discussion, especially if someone happens to think he is being told how *he* ought to behave.

Jesus *speaks* and *acts* with authority, He challenges pride in those who think they 'know it all'. He puts His finger on evil, and when evil is dealt with, peace is discovered. A prayer for today is [2] on page 20.

8

Care for the outcast

Once a leper came and knelt in front of Jesus and begged to be healed. 'If you want to, you can make me well again,' he pleaded.

Jesus, moved with pity, touched him and said, 'I want to. Be healed!' Immediately the leprosy was gone—the man was healed.

Jesus then told him sternly, 'Go and be examined immediately by the Jewish priest. Don't stop to speak to anyone along the way. Take along the offering prescribed by Moses for a leper who is healed, so that everyone will have proof that you are well again.'

But as the man went on his way he began to shout the good news that he was healed; as a result, such crowds soon surrounded Jesus that he could not publicly enter a city anywhere, but had to stay out in the barren wastelands.

Mark chapter 1, verses 40-45

'Oh, no, he's coming over, how can I get away from that tramp?' You may not have spoken such words but you have probably thought them. Outcasts of society can be repugnant to us but Jesus actually touched this leper! His hands stretched out in pity and love.

If we want to love the Jesus way, we must be prepared to do *anything* for *anyone*.

Forgive me, Lord, for being insensitive to the needs of other people.

9

Friendship made plain

Jesus went out to the sea-shore again, . . . he saw Levi, . . . sitting at his tax collection booth. 'Come with me,' Jesus told him. 'Come, be my disciple.' And Levi jumped to his feet and went with him.

That night Levi invited his fellow tax collectors and many other notorious sinners to be his dinner guests so that they could meet Jesus and his disciples . . . But when some of the Jewish religious leaders saw Jesus eating with these men of ill repute, they said to his disciples, 'How can he stand it, to eat with such scum?'

When Jesus heard what they were saying, he told them, 'Sick people need the doctor, not healthy ones! I haven't come to tell good people to repent, but the bad ones.'

Mark chapter 2, verses 13-17

If someone says to you: 'How can Jesus be interested in me? I've done so much wrong and He is so good'—tell them about Levi (also called Matthew), a collaborator with the enemy, one who stole from his own people. Jesus invited *him* to become His disciple.

No one is 'too bad' for Jesus. But, make no mistake, the friendship of Jesus never condones our conduct. He deals with us on *His terms*.

Pray for someone who seems to be 'too bad'.

10
Interest in miracles

Jesus and his disciples withdrew to the beach, followed by a huge crowd . . . For the news about his miracles had spread far and wide and vast numbers came to see him for themselves.

Jesus instructed his disciples to bring around a boat and to have it standing ready to rescue him in case he was crowded off the beach, for there had been many healings that day and as a result great numbers of sick people were crowding around him, trying to touch him.

Mark chapter 3, verses 7-10

'It's a miracle.' These words have been used to describe a winning goal as well as the dramatic recovery of a dangerously ill person. But a true miracle is the work of God and we need to remember:

- When a miracle takes place we must see what it means and say: 'God has done it.'
- The unexpected can happen. When it does, it is meant to lead to a deeper trust in God for all who are involved.
- Jesus doesn't do special 'tricks' for people. He expects us to place our trust in Him, remembering the miracle of His love for us.

'Should I pray for a miracle?' If you are bothered by such a question, share it with a Christian friend, then, together, pray that God will show you what to ask for.

11
Religious mania

When Jesus returned to the house where he was staying, the crowds began to gather again, and soon it was so full of visitors that he couldn't even find time to eat. When his friends heard what was happening they came to try to take him home with them.

'He's out of his mind,' they said.

Now his mother and brothers arrived at the crowded house where he was teaching, and they sent word for him to come out and talk with them. 'Your mother and brothers are outside and want to see you,' he was told.

He replied, 'Who is my mother? Who are my brothers?' Looking at those around him he said, 'These are my mother and brothers! Anyone who does God's will is my brother, and my sister, and my mother.'

Mark chapter 3, verses 20, 21, 31-35

'Faith is all right if it is kept in check.' This is a popular opinion today. Jesus' friends and family thought He was taking His faith far too seriously. They wanted Him to be 'normal'—like everyone else.

But loving God the Jesus way calls for an all-out stand. If we want the *comfort* that faith brings, we must be prepared for the *challenge* of following Jesus.

Ask God for the courage to make a bold stand for Jesus. Use prayer [**3**] on page 20.

12

Panic stations

As evening fell, Jesus said to his disciples, 'Let's cross to the other side of the lake.' . . . But soon a terrible storm arose. High waves began to break into the boat until it was nearly full of water and about to sink.

Jesus was asleep in the stern of the boat with his head on a cushion. Frantically they wakened him, shouting, 'Master, don't you even care that we are all about to drown?'

Then he rebuked the wind and said to the sea, 'Quiet down!' And the wind fell, and there was a great calm. He asked the disciples, 'Why were you so fearful? Don't you even yet have confidence in me?'

And they were filled with awe and said among themselves, 'Who is this man, that even the winds and seas obey him?'

Mark chapter 4, verses 35, 37-41

What are you afraid of most? What kind of situation completely throws you off balance? If you are honest, you know that certain situations cause you to panic.

Is the answer—more faith in Jesus Christ? Probably not! More likely the answer is—use the faith that you already have. Instead of looking desperately for a way of escape, fix your eyes on Jesus Christ and discover that He is in command of every situation.

Talk to God about your fears and anxieties.

13

Just a carpenter?

Soon afterwards Jesus . . . returned with his disciples to Nazareth, his home town. The next Sabbath he went to the synagogue to teach, and the people were astonished at his intellect and his miracles because he was a local man like themselves.

'He's no better than we are,' they said. 'He's just a carpenter, Mary's boy, and a brother of James and Joseph, Judas and Simon. And his sisters live right here among us.' And they were offended.

Then Jesus told them, 'A prophet is honoured everywhere except in his home town and among his relatives and by his own family.' And because of their unbelief he couldn't do any mighty miracles among them except to place his hands on a few sick people and heal them.

Mark chapter 6, verses 1-5

Just a carpenter—with big ideas about himself. Just a clever talker . . . able to tie the religious leaders up in knots. Just an exhibitionist . . . able to do some good tricks.

Times don't change. There always have been people who are eager to pull Jesus down to their own level. But a choice has to be made: Jesus is either a fraud *or* the Son of God. Even if you try to sit on the fence, you are still saying that Jesus cannot be trusted.

Ask God to show you whether you are trusting in the Jesus of your own imagination or in the Jesus revealed to us in the Bible.

14

Slow down . . . speed up

Jesus suggested, 'Let's get away from the crowds for a while and rest.' For so many people were coming and going that they scarcely had time to eat. So they left by boat for a quieter spot. But many people saw them leaving and ran on ahead along the shore and met them as they landed. So the usual vast crowd was there as he stepped from the boat; and he had pity on them because they were like sheep without a shepherd, and he taught them many things they needed to know.

Mark chapter 6, verses 31-34

Christians need to learn that when God tells us to relax He means it for our good. If we relax properly, our health will improve and so will our tempers and our work! Sometimes it is right to say: 'No, I can't do that, I'm busy enough already.'

Or we may be just the opposite, *too* relaxed, in need of speeding up, following the crowd and waiting for things to happen. Jesus challenges us to make a firm decision and declare that we belong to Him. Jesus wants us to use our relaxation time in the *right* way—not always feet up in front of the telly! He suggests a quiet spot with other Christians, relaxing together and talking about the things of God.

Please show me, Lord, whether I need to slow down or speed up. Take control of my relaxation times and teach me to use them wisely.

15

It's not what you eat

Then Jesus called to the crowd to come and hear. 'All of you listen,' he said, 'and try to understand. You aren't harmed by what you eat, but by what you think and say.'

And then he added, 'It is the thought-life that pollutes. For from within, out of men's hearts, come evil thoughts of lust, theft, murder, adultery. Wanting what belongs to others, wickedness, deceit, indecency, envy, slander, pride, and all other folly. All these vile things come from within; they are what pollute you and make you unfit for God.'

Mark chapter 7, verses 14-16, 20-23

John is secretary to the Christian group at work. He has a particular weakness—he likes watching films which he knows don't do him any good. 'I'll go to another town to watch them, that way no one will know,' he thinks.

'The best worker I've ever had,' declared the boss when Liz left for another job. What he didn't know was that she had been helping herself to the petty cash each week. 'Not too much', she had thought, 'just enough to pay for things like make-up and tights—after all, the wages are poor.'

Lord, I realize that You know everything. You know all about those secret sins I manage to hide from others. Forgive me, and give me the strength to resist temptation . . .

16
Mould of your own making?

When the local Jewish leaders learned of Jesus' arrival they came to argue with him.

'Do a miracle for us,' they said. 'Make something happen in the sky. Then we will believe in you.'

His heart fell when he heard this and he said, 'Certainly not. How many more miracles do you people need?'

Mark chapter 8, verses 11, 12

The way some people argue against Jesus makes it obvious that they have already made up their minds not to believe anything He says. It is right to *ask* Jesus questions, but it's also necessary to *accept* His answers.

Others try to strike a bargain with Him. 'If You do this for me, then I'll believe in You.' Jesus put it the other way round: 'You must believe in Me, and then you will discover what I can do for you.'

Often we try to mould Jesus into our image. We accept only what seems fair and reasonable to us, and reject anything that leaves us feeling uncomfortable. But, if we want to know Jesus, we can't dictate our own terms.

Thank the Lord for His patience with you. Ask Him to give you faith and to deal with all your arguments.

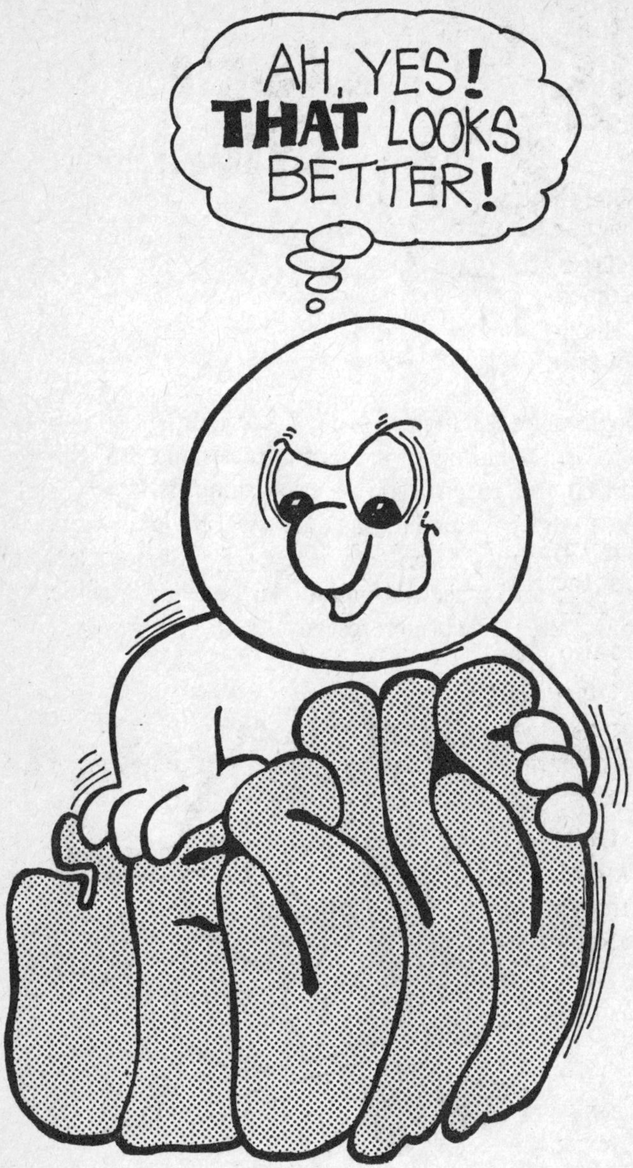
AH, YES! THAT LOOKS BETTER!

EXAMINE the EVIDENCE

Do miracles still happen today? Ask your Christian friends whether they know of modern miracles and probably they will be able to give you several examples. If you talk to some who have undergone successful major hospital surgery, often they describe their recovery as a miracle. Many miracles take place through modern medical facilities that could never have been foreseen a hundred years ago.

The cure of physical and mental disorders, the release of those controlled by demon possession, are all within the power of Jesus Christ. The forces of nature are under His command. Even the dead can be brought back to life. He asks us to accept these miracles as proof that He is the Son of God.

When John the Baptist was imprisoned he sent a message to Jesus enquiring whether He was the Messiah. Jesus replied to the messengers: 'Tell John about the miracles you've seen me do—the blind people that I've healed, the lame people now walking without help, the cured lepers, the deaf who hear, the dead raised to life; and tell him about my preaching the good news to the poor.'

The resurrection of Jesus from the dead is for us the greatest miracle. A similar miracle occurs whenever someone becomes a Christian—a person who has been dead to God receiving new life in Christ. Since God raised Jesus there is no limit to what He can do in this world.

The sceptic may dismiss all miracles as 'fantasy' or 'chance'. The Christian must respond by saying: 'God has done it', whatever the method may be by which God performs a miracle. Miracles are a reminder of God's power and should lead us to worship Him. They point us to a loving, caring God who is active in both ordinary and extraordinary ways.

17
The way in

Once when some mothers were bringing their children to Jesus to bless them, the disciples shooed them away, telling them not to bother him.

But when Jesus saw what was happening he was very displeased with his disciples and said to them, 'Let the children come to me, for the Kingdom of God belongs to such as they. Don't send them away! I tell you as seriously as I know how that anyone who refuses to come to God like a little child will never be allowed into his Kingdom.'

Mark chapter 10, verses 13-15

- Have you noticed the wide-eyed look of a child receiving a present?
- Have you seen a child facing a new situation, nervously gripping a parent's hand?
- Have you realized the depth of a child's trust?

Jesus tells us the secret of the way-in to God's Kingdom. Develop the qualities of little children. Come to Him in simple faith.

Thank Him for His love in sending Jesus into our world. Put your hand in His and go His way, confident that He will never leave you. Trust Him for everything, and, as you get to know more about His reliability, your confidence in His love and power will deepen and nourish your life with joy and happiness.

18

Stand by for a shock

Then it was time for the annual Jewish Passover celebration, and Jesus went to Jerusalem.

After dark one night a Jewish religious leader named Nicodemus, a member of the sect of the Pharisees, came for an interview with Jesus. 'Sir,' he said, 'we all know that God has sent you to teach us. Your miracles are proof enough of this.'

Jesus replied, 'With all the earnestness I possess I tell you this: Unless you are born again, you can never get into the Kingdom of God.'

'Born again!' exclaimed Nicodemus. 'What do you mean? How can an old man go back into his mother's womb and be born again?'

John chapter 2, verse 13, and chapter 3, verses 1-4

It was a shock for Nicodemus to be told that life had to start all over again *if* he wanted a place in God's Kingdom. Like Nicodemus, you may have your own ideas about who Jesus is. 'He is a clever teacher sent by God,' said Nicodemus. But this is not enough. You can *look* at what Jesus did, *listen* to His words, and *agree* they are all good . . . but this does not make you a Christian.

Lord God, help me to learn more about Jesus. Thank You for providing a way for me to enter into Your Kingdom.

Use prayer [12] on page 84.

19
Objections answered

Jesus replied, 'What I am telling you so earnestly is this: Unless one is born of water and the Spirit, he cannot enter the Kingdom of God. Men can only reproduce human life, but the Holy Spirit gives new life from heaven; so don't be surprised at my statement that you must be born again. Just as you can hear the wind but can't tell where it comes from or where it will go next, so it is with the Spirit. We do not know on whom he will next bestow this life from heaven.'

John chapter 3, verses 5-8

There is more to life than food, clothes and work. Jesus speaks of that which cannot be seen—the inner unseen life of the Spirit.

'*I'm too old to change.*' Nicodemus was set in his ways, a major change in his lifestyle may have seemed impossible to him—but not to the Holy Spirit. He can revolutionize anyone's way of life and thinking.

'*I couldn't keep up being a Christian.*' If you think like this, it means you haven't yet realized that to be a Christian means to receive God's power. Although the Spirit is like the wind—you cannot see Him—you will feel the effect of His power.

Lord, You know my hesitations. Help me by Your Spirit to experience Your power.

20

God to the rescue

'And as Moses in the wilderness lifted up the bronze image of a serpent on a pole, even so I must be lifted up upon a pole, so that anyone who believes in me will have eternal life.

For God loved the world so much that he gave his only Son so that anyone who believes in him shall not perish but have eternal life. God did not send his Son into the world to condemn it, but to save it.'

John chapter 3, verses 14-17

If you were drowning, you'd shout for help. If a life-line were thrown to you, you'd be a fool to ignore it. Throughout history God has been throwing out life-lines to people who are 'drowning' in sin. He sent His messengers to warn and show us the way out of difficulties. Finally, Jesus Himself 'jumped into the water to save us'. If we refuse God's life-line, there is no other hope. The Israelites had to turn in faith and look at the bronze serpent in order to be healed.

What do we have to do?

Because of Your love, Lord, I know You reach out to save me day by day. Keep me safe from the attacks of the devil. When I'm tempted to listen to his voice and ignore what You ask of me, please give me the desire to obey You and help me to do so with Your help.

21
Tried and condemned

'There is no eternal doom awaiting those who trust him to save them. But those who don't trust him have already been tried and condemned for not believing in the only Son of God. Their sentence is based on this fact: that the Light from heaven came into the world, but they loved the darkness more than the Light, for their deeds were evil. They hated the heavenly Light because they wanted to sin in the darkness. They stayed away from the Light for fear their sins would be exposed and they would be punished.

John chapter 3, verses 18-20

If I don't trust Jesus to save me, I must accept the consequences.

•*I am condemned.* When I reject His claim to be the Son of God I am sentenced to life in hell.

•*I live in darkness.* If I prefer to remain a prisoner of my sinful habits, refusing to allow Jesus to flood my life with His light, I am sentenced to live with my sin for ever, and bear my own punishment.

Take another look at the Bible reading to see what is the *good* news for those who trust Jesus, and what is the *warning* for those who don't.

Think about the contrast between the light of Jesus and the darkness of sin. Then ask God to flood your life with His light. You might like to use prayer [4] on page 45.

22
Why me?

Inside the city . . . was Bethesda Pool . . .

One of the men lying there had been crippled for thirty-eight years. When Jesus saw him and knew how long he had been ill, he asked him, 'Would you like to get well?'

'I can't,' the man said, 'for I have no one to help me into the pool at the movement of the water. While I am trying to get there, someone else always gets ahead of me.'

Jesus told him, 'Stand up, roll up your sleeping mat and go home!'

Instantly, the man was healed. He rolled up the mat and began walking.

But it was on the Sabbath when this miracle was done.

John chapter 5, verses 2, 5-9

Why should this happen to me? Such a question is never easy to answer. Unfortunately, our circumstances may lead us to indulge in self pity. That's why Jesus asked the cripple whether he *wanted* to get better—he may have preferred to remain ill. On the other hand suffering can bring us closer to God. It's when we are conscious of our own weakness that we learn to depend on God's strength.

Answer Jesus' question: 'Would you like to get well?' Talk to God about your answer.

23
Father and Son

So they began harassing Jesus as a Sabbath-breaker. But Jesus replied, 'My Father constantly does good, and I am following his example.' Then the Jewish leaders were all the more eager to kill him, because in addition to disobeying their Sabbath laws, he had spoken of God as his Father, thereby making himself equal with God.

Jesus replied, 'The Son can do nothing by himself. He does only what he sees the Father doing, and in the same way. For the Father loves the Son, and tells him everything he is doing; and the Son will do far more awesome miracles than this man's healing. He will even raise from the dead anyone he wants to, just as the Father does.'

John chapter 5, verses 16-21

When we become Christians we are adopted into a new family. We can speak to God as 'our Father'. Jesus Christ is our elder brother. Nevertheless Jesus is different from us since He has a unique relationship with God the Father. He is equal with God because He *is* God.

The Jewish leaders wanted to kill Jesus for claiming to be God. Today many people 'kill' Him by ignoring His love and by disobedience to His commands.

Father, help me to recognize the privileges of belonging to Your family. Give me the desire to accept the responsibilities that are mine.

24
After death—what?

'I say emphatically that anyone who listens to my message and believes in God who sent me has eternal life, and will never be damned for his sins, but has already passed out of death into life. And I solemnly declare that the time is coming, in fact it is here, when the dead shall hear my voice—the voice of the Son of God—and those who listen shall live. The Father has life in himself, and has granted his Son to have life in himself, and to judge the sins of all mankind because he is the Son of Man. But I pass no judgment without consulting the Father. I judge as I am told. And my judgment is absolutely fair and just, for it is according to the will of God who sent me and is not merely my own.'

John chapter 5, verses 24-27, 30

Death is a conversation stopper. If someone starts to talk about death, it isn't long before someone else changes the subject. It's taboo because our materialistic society hasn't got an answer to it. But Jesus has! Death is not the end, as some people would lead us to believe, it is a gateway, either to life in the presence of God or to judgment and punishment for unforgiven sin. What we do with Jesus *now* is the dividing line.

Thank you, Lord Jesus, for taking the punishment for my sins when You died on the cross, and for making death the gateway to life.

25

Truth under attack

Some of the people who lived there in Jerusalem said among themselves, 'Isn't this the man they are trying to kill? But here he is preaching in public, and they say nothing to him. Can it be that our leaders have learned, after all, that he really is the Messiah? But how could he be? For we know where this man was born; when Christ comes, he will just appear and no one will know where he comes from.'

So Jesus, in a sermon in the Temple, called out, 'Yes, you know me and where I was born and brought up, but I am the representative of one you don't know, and he is Truth. I know him because I was with him, and he sent me to you.'

Then the Jewish leaders sought to arrest him; but no hand was laid on him, for God's time had not yet come.

John chapter 7, verses 25-30

Jealousy and misunderstanding always cause untold disruption of God's work. Because of it the glory of Jesus is dimmed in many churches. The Jewish leaders were jealous of Jesus' popularity and power. It made them want to kill Him.

Jesus, the representative of the Truth, puts His finger on the sin in our lives. He condemns jealousy and pride. He questions prejudice. He demands loyalty and love first towards God but also to all those who follow Him.

Think, then pray: God's finger is pointing at me.

26
Arrested!

Many among the crowds at the Temple believed on Jesus. 'After all,' they said, 'what miracles do you expect the Messiah to do that this man hasn't done?'

When the Pharisees heard that the crowds were in this mood, they and the chief priests sent officers to arrest Jesus. But Jesus told them, '(Not yet!) I am to be here a little longer. Then I shall return to the one who sent me. You will search for me but not find me. And you won't be able to come where I am.'

John chapter 7, verses 31-34

Why couldn't the officers carry out the arrest? Was it the look on Jesus' face that 'arrested' them instead? Was it the 'not yet' that carried such conviction that they were rendered powerless?

We need to allow the full impact of Jesus' personality to stop thoughtless words, to control bad temper and to arrest our hasty actions. If we are constantly looking to Him, we will come to recognize His commands.

Lord, make me a person of good temper, so that even when I am provoked I remain calm. Give me Your peace as I trust in You. Help me to be able to recognize Your commands, and allow Your firmness to become my strength.

2 PRAYER PAGE

Going all the way

4 Total commitment

Prayer of commitment (*for use if you seriously want to become a Christian*): You know me, Father. I can't pull the wool over Your eyes. So far I know I've put off thinking about all that Christ did for me. Now I ask You to forgive my sin, help me to turn from it and to acknowledge Jesus Christ as my Saviour and Lord.

Prayer of dedication: Thank You, Lord, for the new friends I have because I am a Christian. Show us the need to play our part in encouraging each other to go the Jesus way.

(21, page 39)

5 When courage is needed

Thank You, Father, for all the brave followers of Jesus Christ who have been willing to risk everything for Him. I'm aware of situations that frighten me, and I ask that You'll give me courage to speak out for You.

(27, page 46)

6 Asking for God's strength

Lord, sometimes, because I feel fit and healthy and capable of anything, I try to manage on my own, but there are times when I realize how weak I really am. Help me to see that only by relying on You can I find *real* strength.

(80, page 123)

27
No turning back

The Temple police who had been sent to arrest Jesus returned to the chief priests and Pharisees. 'Why didn't you bring him in?' they demanded.

'He says such wonderful things!' they mumbled. 'We've never heard anything like it.'

'So you also have been led astray?' the Pharisees mocked. 'Is there a single one of us Jewish rulers or Pharisees who believes he is the Messiah? These stupid crowds do, yes; but what do they know about it? A curse upon them anyway!'

Then Nicodemus spoke up ... 'Is it legal to convict a man before he is even tried?' he asked. They replied, 'Are you a wretched Galilean too? Search the Scriptures and see for yourself—no prophets will come from Galilee!'

John chapter 7, verses 45-52

You cannot hide the fact that you are a follower of Christ. The first time you openly say, 'I'm a Christian,' you experience the joy and relief of having let your secret out into the open and the awareness that you cannot turn back.

But this stand has to be taken in front of enemies as well as friends. Colleagues at work, neighbours and relatives may resent you and what you say, but, if you are consistent, you will gain their respect.

Prayer [5] on page 45 or prayer [17] on page 122.

YEAH, HE'S A CHRISTIAN...
I HEARD HIM SAY SO!...

28

Never too busy

A man came running to Jesus and knelt down and asked, 'Good Teacher, what must I do to get to heaven?'

'Why do you call me good?' Jesus asked. 'Only God is truly good. But as for your question—you know the commandments: don't kill, don't commit adultery, don't steal, don't lie, don't cheat, respect your father and mother.'

'Sir, I've never once broken a single one of those laws,' the man replied.

Jesus felt genuine love for this man as he looked at him. 'You lack only one thing,' he told him; 'go and sell all you have and give the money to the poor—and you shall have treasure in heaven—and come, follow me.'

Then the man's face fell, and he went sadly away, for he was very rich.

Mark chapter 10, verses 17-22

If someone comes to see you unexpectedly, asking for advice, what do you think? 'Not so and so again,' or, 'I wish I'd gone out earlier'.

Jesus *always* has time for people. When we come to Him His complete attention is given. And He always knows exactly what the trouble is. We may not get the answers we would like, or the easy way out of a sticky problem, but He will always give the *best* advice and expect us to take it. Even if we don't respond, He still loves us. But holding back from Him will keep us off the road of discipleship and on the road to disappointment and failure.

29
Bad news?

Now they were on the way to Jerusalem . . .

Taking them aside, Jesus once more began describing all that was going to happen to him when they arrived at Jerusalem.

'When we get there,' he told them, 'I, the Son of Mankind, will be arrested and taken before the chief priests and the Jewish leaders, who will sentence me to die and hand me over to the Romans to be killed. They will mock me and spit on me and flog me with their whips and kill me; but after three days I will come back to life again.'

Mark chapter 10, verses 32-34

The shock of bad news often causes people to switch off before they have heard all the details. The disciples were no exception. Although Jesus repeatedly told them about His death and resurrection, it was only after the events that they appreciated what He had said.

Our faith is not based on a man who merely talked and went around doing good. He proved His words by what He did. His love for us made Him willing to die on the cross. Don't despair, He isn't a dead figure on a crucifix—He is our living Lord.

Lord, please forgive me when I'm deaf to Your voice. Help me to listen to You and to act on what You say.

30

Out of hand

When they arrived back in Jerusalem Jesus went to the Temple and began to drive out the merchants and their customers, and knocked over the tables of the money-changers and the stalls of those selling doves, and stopped everyone from bringing in loads of merchandise.

He told them, 'It is written in the Scriptures, "My Temple is to be a place of prayer for all nations," but you have turned it into a den of robbers.'

Mark chapter 11, verses 15-17

A large business empire had sprung up in the Temple and the corruption that came with it affected even the priests. No one had the courage or concern to do anything about the dishonesty—until Jesus arrived.

We may not be guilty of robbing people; although what about that 'borrowed' record? But we are guilty of robbing God. 'I've got too many things to do today—no time to pray.' If worship and prayer are repeatedly crowded out of our lives, gradually we lose contact with God. We must learn to say 'no' firmly to some of our activities, including 'good' ones.

I confess, Lord, that often I waste time that could be used for prayer. I watch the telly for hours, idly chat with friends . . . Show me how to discipline my life so that I do not miss spending time with You.

31

I won't believe because . . .

As Jesus was walking through the Temple area, the chief priests and other Jewish leaders came up to him demanding, 'What's going on here? Who gave you the authority to drive out the merchants?'

Jesus replied, 'I'll tell you if you answer one question. What about John the Baptist? Was he sent by God, or not? Answer me!'

They talked it over among themselves. 'If we reply that God sent him, then he will say, "All right, why didn't you accept him?" But if we say God didn't send him, then the people will start a riot.' (For the people all believed strongly that John was a prophet.) So they said, 'We can't answer. We don't know.'

To which Jesus replied, 'Then I won't answer your question either!'

Mark chapter 11, verses 27-33

- How do I know the Bible is true?
- How can I know which church is right when they are all divided?
- I live a good life. Why do I need to go to church?
- Why does God allow so much pain?

You've probably faced questions like these. However well you answer, your friends will not automatically believe. They may be like the Jewish leaders with minds made up to reject what Jesus said. Pride is often the real problem, and stubborn wills that need to be broken.

Ask God for humility and faith.

32
Punch line

Jesus said, 'A man planted a vineyard and built a wall around it and dug a pit for pressing out the grape juice, and built a watchman's tower. Then he leased the farm to tenant farmers and went on a trip to a distant land. At harvest time he sent one of his men to collect his share of the crop. But the farmers beat up the man and sent him back empty-handed.

'The owner then sent another of his men, who received the same treatment, only worse, for his head was seriously injured. The next man he sent was killed; and later, others were either beaten or killed, until there was only one left—his only son. He finally sent him, thinking they would surely give him their full respect.

'But . . . they caught him and murdered him.'

The Jewish leaders wanted to arrest him then and there . . . for they knew he was pointing at them . . . —But they were afraid to touch him for fear of a mob.

Mark chapter 12, verses 2-8, 12

If you read this story and think, 'It's nothing to do with me. It's about the failure of the Jewish leaders to accept Jesus,' then you've missed the punch line!

Think, then pray: I betray Jesus—when I proudly refuse to acknowledge, 'I'm wrong', when I behave in a way that makes people say, 'I thought he was supposed to be a Christian!'

33
Tricky situation

They sent other religious and political leaders to talk with Jesus and try to trap him into saying something he could be arrested for.

'Teacher', these spies said, 'we know you fearlessly tell the truth! You aren't influenced by the opinions and desires of men, but sincerely teach the ways of God. Now tell us, is it right to pay taxes to Rome, or not?'

Jesus saw their trick and said, 'Show me a coin and I'll tell you.'

When they handed it to him he asked, 'Whose picture and title is this on the coin?' They replied, 'The emperor's.'

'All right,' he said, 'if it is his, give it to him. But everything that belongs to God must be given to God!' And they scratched their heads in bafflement at his reply.

Mark chapter 12, verses 13-17

Challenged by a crowd of religious authorities, Jesus refused to back down. They planned to discredit Him in front of the people. But their plan backfired and they found themselves under attack.

Jesus still puts His finger on sore spots and challenges us to face up to their effect on both ourselves and others.

Lord, I know there are things I do/say/think that You could put Your finger on. Please do this now, and give me Your power to act on Your truth.

34
Priorities straightened out

One of the teachers of religion . . . asked, 'Of all the commandments, which is the most important?'

Jesus replied, 'The one that says, "Hear, O Israel! The Lord our God is the one and only God. And you must love him with all your heart and soul and mind and strength."

'The second is: "You must love others as much as yourself." No other commandments are greater than these.'

The teacher of religion replied, 'Sir, you have spoken a true word in saying that there is only one God and no other. And I know it is far more important to love him with all my heart and understanding and strength, and to love others as myself, than to offer all kinds of sacrifices on the altar of the Temple.'

Realizing this man's understanding, Jesus said to him, 'You are not far from the Kingdom of God.'

Mark chapter 12, verses 28-34

Are you ever in danger of becoming bogged down in the less important details of the Christian faith? The religious leaders had been asking their hair-splitting questions. They wanted their faith reduced to a set of rules. Then someone asked a refreshingly honest question. Jesus answered by summarizing the commandments, joining together *true* love for God with *real* love for others. When such love is the mainspring of your life you also will be able to get your priorities straight. Use prayer [8] on page 75.

35
Beware!

Jesus taught: 'Beware of the teachers of religion! For they love to wear the robes of the rich and scholarly, and to have everyone bow to them as they walk through the markets. They love to sit in the best seats in the synagogues, and at the places of honour at banquets—but they shamelessly cheat widows out of their homes and then, to cover up the kind of men they really are, they pretend to be pious by praying long prayers in public. Because of this, their punishment will be the greater.'

Mark chapter 12, verses 38-40

'Don't do as I do, do as I say.' These words, often said as a joke, reveal the wide gap between what we know to be right and what we actually do. Often we're ashamed because we fail to live up to our standards. We hesitate to talk about other people's faults because we are all too conscious of our own. But Jesus was different. His words and deeds *did* match up so He was able to point out the failures of the religious leaders.

There are times when we are tempted to compare ourselves with other people and to boast of our own goodness. It's harder, but more useful, to ask God to show us ourselves as we really are.

Lord, as I begin to see how real and frightening my sins are, I know I need to ask for more of Jesus' forgiveness.

36
Where the money goes

Then Jesus went over to the collection boxes in the Temple and sat and watched as the crowds dropped in their money. Some who were rich put in large amounts. Then a poor widow came and dropped in two pennies.

He called his disciples to him and remarked, 'That poor widow has given more than all those rich men put together! For they gave a little of their surplus, while she gave up her last penny.'

Mark chapter 12, verses 41-44

What am I saying to God when I give my money?

'You can have what is left after I've bought everything else I need.'

'I'll give my fair share just as long as everybody else does.'

'Thank You, Lord, for my rise in income. I want to give You more.'

Jesus does not measure giving by the large amounts a person gives—but by how much is held back for private use. In your regular giving do you support ... your church fellowship? ... missionary societies and missionaries known to you personally? ... worldwide relief organizations?

Honesty Spot • Do I give cheerfully and willingly? Does my giving reveal how much I trust God?

Help me, Lord, to be generous in my giving and in all my dealings with people.

...HERE, LORD! YOU NEED IT MORE THAN I DO!...
GOD
ME

GIVERS AND GRABBERS

Where money is concerned our society is made up of two main groups—the givers and the grabbers.

The *first* group think in terms of giving satisfaction by doing a job thoroughly and being of service to others. The *second* group is concerned only with such questions as—'What is in it for me?'—'How can I get the *biggest* financial reward for the *least* amount of effort?'

Some people advise a mixture of both attitudes, but often it is one of these outlooks that wins out and influences the whole pattern of life. The Christian's attitude to possessions and money should be that *both* are gifts from God, on trust from Him to be used in His service.

Recognizing our duty to our own church fellowship, and giving regularly to the Lord's work is loving the Jesus way. And don't forget the missionary societies at work in this country and abroad.

Worldwide relief organizations focus attention on the needs of the third world. But, linked with the giving of money, there must be a real spirit of generosity and involvement in prayer: giving and praying must go hand in hand.

Giving hospitality is another practical way of loving the Jesus way. What about that lonely person who lives next door or attends your church? A friendly invitation to your home would be most appreciated. An opportunity to share in normal family life is always welcome. Don't be put off if your neighbours refuse you; look around and ask God to show you those that want your help.

Working with people who have specialized needs may be your gift. Check with your local voluntary social service organization for information. The task seems to be daunting? Then ask a friend to share the entertaining and hospitality with you.

'Adopting' a grandma and/or grandad is another way of extending your family. Many lonely grandparents whose families can only visit them occasionally would welcome the opportunity to get to know young children and even act as babysitters.

Once you've learnt to love the Jesus way by opening the door of your home—you will need to get a diary to keep track of your engagements!

37

Seeing below the surface

Jesus was in Bethany, at the home of Simon the leper; during supper a woman came in with a beautiful flask of expensive perfume. Then, breaking the seal, she poured it over his head. Some of those at the table were indignant among themselves about this 'waste' as they called it.

'Why, she could have sold that perfume for a fortune and given the money to the poor!' they snarled.

But Jesus said, 'Let her alone; why criticize her for doing a good thing? You always have the poor among you, and they badly need your help, and you can aid them whenever you want to; but I won't be here much longer.

'She has done what she could, and has anointed my body beforehand for burial. And I tell you this in solemn truth, that wherever the Good News is preached throughout the world, this woman's deed will be remembered and praised.'

Mark chapter 14, verses 3-9

Being able to see below the surface of an action can give pleasure or pain, depending on the motives of the one observed. Jesus understood the motives of Simon and the woman . . . and He knows the reason for *our* actions.

Lord, forgive me for the times when I have tried to pull the wool over Your eyes. I know I have done things just for my own glory, seeking approval from those around rather than from You.

38

When you feel lost

'I am the Good Shepherd. The Good Shepherd lays down his life for the sheep. A hired man will run when he sees a wolf coming and will leave the sheep, for they aren't his and he isn't their shepherd . . . The hired man runs because he is hired and has no real concern for the sheep.

'I am the Good Shepherd and know my own sheep, and they know me, just as my Father knows me and I know the Father; and I lay down my life for the sheep.'

John chapter 10, verses 11-15

Travelling on a crowded train, or walking across an empty moor, you may experience the same feeling, 'I'm all alone'. Perhaps you want to add, 'And no one seems to care.' Jesus reassures us of His love and care—each one of His followers is important to Him.

A shepherd's job includes:

- finding food and water for the flock.
- offering protection in times of danger.
- daily care for the well-being of the sheep.

Whenever you say the Lord's prayer you are asking for this kind of help. Your Heavenly Father will give it to you as He has promised. For Jesus the Good Shepherd gave His own life for us—that's the measure of His love.

Thank Jesus for dying for you.

39

Proof already given

It was winter, and Jesus was in Jerusalem at the time of the Dedication Celebration. He was at the Temple, walking through the section known as Solomon's Hall. The Jewish leaders surrounded him and asked, 'How long are you going to keep us in suspense? If you are the Messiah, tell us plainly.'

'I have already told you, and you didn't believe me,' Jesus replied. 'The proof is in the miracles I do in the name of my Father. But you don't believe me because you are not part of my flock.'

John chapter 10, verses 22-26

The religious leaders refused to accept the proof that Jesus had already given them. They were like children with blindfolds on. Notice the name of the place where they ganged up on Jesus. It was a pity that the wisdom of Solomon was not evident in their thinking.

This is the only time the Feast of Dedication/Hannukah is mentioned in the New Testament. It often coincides with Christmas. At this time the Jews remember the cleansing and dedication of the Temple after it had been profaned in 167 BC. It is interesting that early Christians saw a vital link between the Feast of Dedication and the day when Christ was born—on the one hand a temple made with hands, on the other, the living Temple of God come down from Heaven to live among us.

40

Danger . . . ungrateful people

'My sheep recognize my voice, and I know them, and they follow me. I give them eternal life and they shall never perish. No one shall snatch them away from me, for my Father has given them to me, and he is more powerful than anyone else, so no one can kidnap them from me. I and the Father are one.'

Then again the Jewish leaders picked up stones to kill him.

Jesus said, 'At God's direction I have done many a miracle to help the people. For which one are you killing me?'

They replied, 'Not for any good work, but for blasphemy; you, a mere man, have declared yourself to be God.'

John chapter 10, verses 27-33

Do you realize how many privileges are yours if you are going the Jesus way?

• *A new relationship*. Jesus puts you in touch with God and you can talk to Him at any time.

• *A new unending life*. Each day you can be forgiven by God, and experience a freedom from anxiety. Even death can be faced with confidence.

• *A new security*. When you fail Him, God won't let you go. You inherit the promises He made, including this one: 'I am with you always.'

Help me, Father, to understand and appreciate all that belongs to me as a Christian.

41

To be a servant

Jesus knew on the evening of Passover Day that it would be his last night on earth before returning to his Father. During supper the Devil had already suggested to Judas Iscariot . . . that this was the night to carry out his plan to betray Jesus . . . And how he (Jesus) loved his disciples! So he got up from the supper table, took off his robe, wrapped a towel around his loins, poured water into a basin and began to wash the disciples' feet and to wipe them with the towel he had around him.

John chapter 13, verses 1-5

There are some jobs we resent having to do because we have an inflated view of ourselves. We may not have exactly said, 'It's beneath my dignity to do such a job,' but most of us have thought along these lines on some occasion.

The disciples were dumbfounded at what Jesus did. He acted like an ordinary slave and put everyone to shame by His uncomplaining attitude. His love for them had always shone through what He did. Now, as he faced His greatest test, His concern for them did not lessen. He had not come to be served, but to help others. He did not regard His own satisfaction as a right. His life was one of *giving* right to the end.

Thank You, Lord, for the humility of Jesus. Help me to remember that I have to be helped by Him before I can serve others.

42

Easier said than done

After washing their feet he put on his robe again and sat down and asked, 'Do you understand what I was doing? You call me "Master" and "Lord," and you do well to say it, for it is true. And since I, the Lord and Teacher, have washed your feet, you ought to wash each other's feet.

'I have given you an example to follow: do as I have done to you.

'How true it is that a servant is not greater than his master. Nor is the messenger more important than the one who sends him. You know these things—now do them. That is the path of blessing.'

John chapter 13, verses 12-17

'All talk and no action,' may well describe some Christians. On the other hand, there are those who are practical and helpful, but fail to point out that the good they do is inspired by God.

How can we close the gap between saying and doing?

Ask God to show you what stops you helping other people. It may be pride, laziness or selfishness. And the same things may make it difficult for you to talk to others about Jesus.

Make a short list (a long one will just put you off) either of people to visit or of jobs to do for someone. Make up your mind to take some action within the next week.

43

Love that rings true

As soon as Judas left the room, Jesus said, 'My time has come; the glory of God will soon surround me—and God shall receive great praise because of all that happens to me. And God shall give me his own glory, and this so very soon. Dear, dear children, how brief are these moments before I must go away and leave you! Then, though you search for me, you cannot come to me—just as I told the Jewish leaders.

'And so I am giving a new commandment to you now—love each other just as much as I love you. Your strong love for each other will prove to the world that you are my disciples.'

John chapter 13, verses 31-35

You can see how genuine a Christian's faith is by the quality and depth of love that is produced. 'Love one another just as much as I love you,' is the command Jesus gives His followers. When we are full of joy we should let others share the benefits. If we are in difficulties, we shouldn't withdraw into our shells, thinking only about ourselves. Instead we should still try to help other people with *their* problems.

Love like this comes only from Jesus. It can overcome *all* obstacles, breaking down the barriers of colour and social background.

Ask God to help you to love others as much as Jesus loves you.

44

Recipes for happiness

'I have loved you even as the Father has loved me. Live within my love. When you obey me you are living in my love, just as I obey my Father and live in his love. I have told you this so that you will be filled with my joy. Yes, your cup of joy will overflow! I demand that you love each other as much as I love you. And here is how to measure it—the greatest love is shown when a person lays down his life for his friends; and you are my friends if you obey me. I no longer call you slaves, for a master doesn't confide in his slaves; now you are my friends, proved by the fact that I have told you everything the Father told me.'

John chapter 15, verses 9-15

'Do your own thing.' 'Enjoy yourself while you can.' But it has been said that if you search for happiness, you will never find it. It only comes as a by-product, when you are busy doing something else. The only way to happiness is:

- to remember that Jesus Christ loves you and wants the best for you.
- to obey Him . . . doing what He says, no matter what.
- to care for other people . . . always putting their needs before your own, and giving willingly of your time.

Forgive me, Father, when I'm so influenced by the way of the world around me that I neglect the way of Jesus Christ, Your Son.

45

Appointed for persecution?

'You didn't choose me. I chose you. I appointed you to go and produce good fruit always, so that no matter what you ask for from the Father, using my name, he will give it to you.

'I demand that you love each other, for you get enough hate from the world. But then, it hated me before it hated you. The world would love you if you belonged to it; but you don't—for I chose you to come out of the world, and so it hates you. Do you remember what I told you? "A slave isn't greater than his master!" So since they persecuted me, naturally they will persecute you. And if they had listened to me, they would listen to you. The people of the world will persecute you because you belong to me, for they don't know God who sent me.'

John chapter 15, verses 16-21

Being laughed at by work-mates; imprisonment by the State—persecution takes many forms. But Jesus warned His followers that they would be persecuted. Therefore their love for one another was of great importance.

You can help persecuted Christians by

- getting hold of reliable information and praying for them.
- writing letters to them and to their relatives.

Can you think of any other ways?

Talk to God about the persecution you have to face for Him, and the love you have to show for Him.

46

Prepared for attack

After saying these things Jesus crossed the Kidron ravine with his disciples and entered a grove of olive trees. Judas, the betrayer, knew this place, for Jesus had gone there many times with his disciples.

The chief priests and Pharisees had given Judas a squad of soldiers and police to accompany him. Now with blazing torches, lanterns, and weapons they arrived at the olive grove.

Jesus fully realized all that was going to happen to him. Stepping forward to meet them he asked, 'Whom are you looking for?'

'Jesus of Nazareth,' they replied.

'I am he,' Jesus said . . .

So the Jewish police with the soldiers and their lieutenant arrested Jesus and tied him.

John chapter 18, verses 1-6, 12

Often we're caught out, unprepared for the turn of events. 'If only I'd been ready,' we think afterwards. Jesus had prepared Himself for this arrest and He'd warned His followers of what would happen. Immediately before the arrest He had been praying—He was ready. In complete control of the situation, Jesus gave Himself up, then, calmly, negotiated the release of the panic-stricken disciples.

'Whom are you looking for?' Jesus asked the soldiers—and He asks *us* the same question.

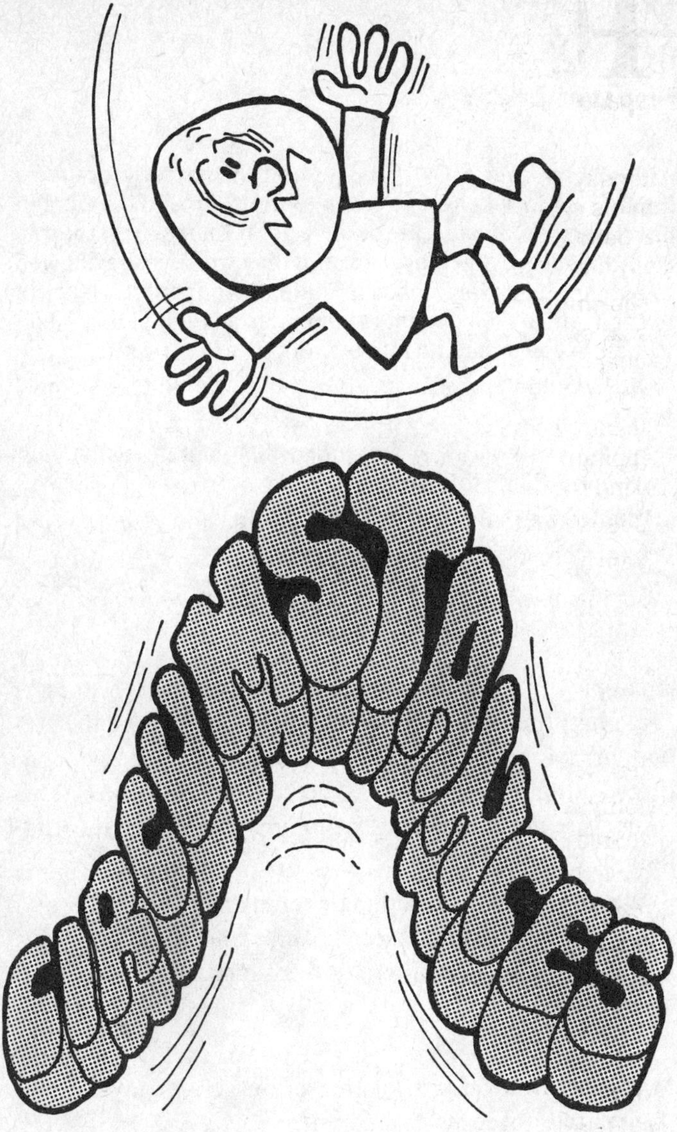
CIRCUMSTANCES

47

Denial of justice

Jesus' trial before Caiaphas ended in the early hours of the morning. Next he was taken to the palace of the Roman governor. His accusers wouldn't go in themselves for that would 'defile' them, they said, and they wouldn't be allowed to eat the Passover lamb. So Pilate, the governor, went out to them and asked, 'What is your charge against this man? What are you accusing him of doing?'

'We wouldn't have arrested him if he weren't a criminal,' they retorted.

'Then take him away and judge him yourselves by your own laws,' Pilate told them.

'But we want him crucified,' they said, 'and your approval is required.'

John chapter 18, verses 28-31

A couple of rigged trials involving contradictory witnesses —at night-time, too, which was illegal—these were the preliminaries to the show-down before Pilate. Although concerned about their religious defilement, the accusers of Jesus were not ashamed of being involved in the most infamous crime in history.

Whenever we do something wrong, unless we repent and stop, we become entangled in more and more evil. Lies lead to fresh lies, and bitterness feeds on hatred.

Make me aware, Lord, of the seriousness of my sin and the greatness of Jesus' love for me.

48

Not guilty but . . .

Then Pilate laid open Jesus' back with a leaded whip, and the soldiers made a crown of thorns and placed it on his head and robed him in royal purple. 'Hail, King of the Jews!' they mocked, and struck him with their fists.

Pilate went outside again and said to the Jews, 'I am going to bring him out to you now, but understand clearly that I find him not guilty.'

Then Jesus came out wearing the crown of thorns and the purple robe. And Pilate said, 'Behold the man!'

At sight of him the chief priests and Jewish officials began yelling, 'Crucify! Crucify!'

'You crucify him,' Pilate said. 'I find him not guilty.'

They replied, 'By our laws he ought to die because he called himself the Son of God.'

John chapter 19, verses 1-7

Jesus was no trouble-maker, and Pilate knew it! But the Governor lacked the courage of his convictions and instead acted on impulse. He decided that the death of *one* innocent person was infinitely preferable to a riot.

Probe Spot • Am I like Pilate . . . believing one thing and doing the opposite? Do I stick to my principles . . . even when the cost is great?

Thank You, Father, for the courage of Jesus.

49
King Jesus

It was now about noon of the day before Passover. And Pilate said to the Jews, 'Here is your king!'

'Away with him,' they yelled, 'away with him—crucify him!'

'What? Crucify your king?' Pilate asked.

'We have no king but Caesar,' the chief priests shouted back.

Then Pilate gave Jesus to them to be crucified.

So they had him at last, and he was taken out of the city, carrying his cross to the place known as 'The Skull,' in Hebrew, 'Golgotha.' There they crucified him . . . And Pilate posted a sign over him reading, 'JESUS OF NAZARETH, THE KING OF THE JEWS.'

John chapter 19, verses 14-19

Written in three popular languages, it was a sign for everyone to read. Ironically, Pilate's final verdict was the accurate one. 'Jesus'—the man who was different—shook the foundations of religious tradition and men's ideas about God. He perfectly shows us the love of God because He *is* the Son of God.

'The King of the Jews'—but Jesus is more than this. He is the KING of kings and LORD of lords—nailed to a roughly made cross for you and me.

Prayer [10] on page 84 is for today.

3 PRAYER PAGE

Living every day the Jesus way

7 Being honest with myself

I can spot other people's mistakes a mile off, yet I find difficulty in recognizing my own. Show me my faults, Lord; I turn to You for forgiveness.

(70, page 107)

8 The greatness of God

Almighty God, how I need to be reminded of Your greatness! So often petty things obsess me—I need a clearer vision of what really matters. Let Your love liberate my life, and rub off on to the people I meet.

(34, page 54)

9 Prayer gives power

Lord Jesus, You were ready because You spent so much time in prayer. You made events fit in with Your praying, while I seem to fit in my praying as and when the mood takes me. Teach me more about the power of prayer and of my need to talk to God my Father about everything.

(77, page 118)

PRAY DAILY

50

Missing the mark

Two robbers were also crucified that morning, their crosses on either side of his. And so the Scripture was fulfilled that said, 'He was counted among evil men.'

The people jeered at him as they walked by, and wagged their heads in mockery.

'Ha! Look at you now!' they yelled at him. 'So, you can destroy the Temple and rebuild it in three days! If you're so wonderful, save yourself and come down from the cross.'

The chief priests and religious leaders were also standing around joking about Jesus.

'He's quite clever at "saving" others,' they said, 'but he can't save himself!'

'Hey there, Messiah!' they shouted at him. 'You "King of Israel!" Come on down from the cross and we'll believe you!'

And even the two robbers dying with him cursed him.

Mark chapter 15, verses 27-32

- If I disbelieve the words of Jesus . . .
- If I refuse to see that He died for me . . .
- If I'm cynical about Him, saying: 'He's no different, we all have to die . . .' then I've missed the mark.

Jesus spoke of Himself as the 'Temple', saying that although He would be destroyed He would return to life on the third day. He chose the harder way and stayed on the cross to complete His work as Saviour. Use prayer [11] on page 84.

20
1
5
9
18
11
6
15
17
3

51

Getting the point

About noon, darkness fell across the entire land, lasting until three o'clock that afternoon.

Then Jesus called out with a loud voice, 'Eli, Eli, lama sabachthani?' ('My God, my God, why have you deserted me?')

Some of the people standing there thought he was calling for the prophet Elijah. So one man ran and got a sponge and filled it with sour wine and held it up to him on a stick.

'Let's see if Elijah will come and take him down!' he said.

Then Jesus uttered another loud cry, and dismissed his spirit.

And the curtain in the Temple was split apart from top to bottom.

When the Roman officer standing beside his cross saw how he dismissed his spirit, he exclaimed, 'Truly, this was a son of God!'

Mark chapter 15, verses 33-39

A tough, professional soldier, who had seen many people die, realized that Jesus was not just another criminal. There was something about this man that made him take notice.

While the followers of Jesus were keeping their distance this officer was the first person to acknowledge Jesus after His death. Later in the barrack-room he probably had a tough time explaining what he had said. If you agree with his verdict, ask God to help you to tell someone else about Jesus Christ.

52

The cost of Jesus living

Afterwards Joseph of Arimathea, who had been a secret disciple of Jesus for fear of the Jewish leaders, boldly asked Pilate for permission to take Jesus' body down; and Pilate told him to go ahead. So he came and took it away.

Nicodemus, the man who had come to Jesus at night, came too, bringing a hundred pounds of embalming ointment made from myrrh and aloes. Together they wrapped Jesus' body in a long linen cloth saturated with the spices, as is the Jewish custom of burial. The place of crucifixion was near a grove of trees, where there was a new tomb, never used before. And so, because of the need for haste before the Sabbath, and because the tomb was close at hand, they laid him there.

John chapter 19, verses 38-42

Every day you make decisions of one kind or another. But whenever you make an important one, there is the moment of doubt. We've met Nicodemus before (*see 18, 19, 27*). Now he stands by his decision to speak up for Jesus.

Living for Jesus involves more than words. Your deeds must back up what you say. There is a personal cost involved as well. Nicodemus may have lost the opportunity for any further promotion. Sacrifice is at the centre of living the Jesus way.

Pray about any decisions you know you will have to make this week.

53
Alive!

Early Sunday morning, while it was still dark, Mary Magdalene came to the tomb and found that the stone was rolled aside from the entrance.

She glanced over her shoulder and saw someone standing behind her. It was Jesus, but she didn't recognize him.

'Why are you crying?' he asked her. 'Whom are you looking for?' (She thought he was the gardener.)

'Sir,' she said, 'if you have taken him away, tell me where you have put him, and I will go and get him.'

'Mary!' Jesus said. She turned towards him.

'Master!' she exclaimed.

John chapter 20, verses 1, 14-16

Mary owed Jesus a great debt. He had cured her of demon-possession. She had travelled from Galilee, watched the crucifixion from a distance, was present at the burial, and now had come to embalm the body. When she found that the body was missing confusion was added to her grief.

There are times when it seems as if our whole world is collapsing around us. To survive we need the certainty that comes from having met the risen Jesus. His victory over death is a real assurance of His power to help us.

Ask God to make you aware of the tremendous power of Jesus Christ.

54

Confidence for the future

That evening the disciples were meeting behind locked doors, in fear of the Jewish leaders, when suddenly Jesus was standing there among them. After greeting them, he showed them his hands and side. And how wonderful was their joy as they saw their Lord!

He spoke to them again and said, 'As the Father has sent me, even so I am sending you.'

John chapter 20, verses 19-21

Given time most people can adjust to bad news, but living with uncertainty is a great strain. You may be constantly troubled by such questions as, 'Is my job safe?' Or: 'How can I be sure of his/her love; I may be let down?'

What's the answer to all these problems? 'Don't worry, it may never happen.' Or: 'You need more faith?'

The disciples were totally disheartened. Not sure whether Jesus was dead or alive, they knew it was possible that they were the next ones earmarked for execution.

Stepping right into confusion, Jesus completely transforms tense situations. He brings confidence and a new direction. He offers a new dimension to life, hope instead of despair. The resurrection means there is always a future with Jesus, whatever problems you have to face. Prayer [16] on page 122 is for today.

55

Trust and be sure

Jesus' disciples saw him do many other miracles besides the ones written in this book, but these are recorded so that you will believe that he is the Messiah, the Son of God, and that believing in him you will have Life.

John chapter 20, verses 30, 31

Becoming a Christian is rather like getting married. After a period of becoming acquainted, which may be short or long, there comes the wedding—the moment of complete commitment.

Are you committed to the Jesus of your own imagination or to the Jesus who:

- lived a real human life, and, although tempted, never sinned?
- offered His life as a sacrifice for sin?
- conquered death and came back to life again, demonstrating God's mighty power?

Some marriages run into trouble because the partners don't work at the marriage. Each one is concerned with his/her own pleasure. God's partners must be concerned with pleasing Him and never settle back after the initial commitment. Each day our trust is put to the test in different ways. And how you cope with that crisis at work, or how you react to those who rub you up the wrong way matters to God.

Thank You, Father, for the great adventure of the Christian life. I know that You will travel with me wherever I go.

COME ON, SON! IT'S QUITE SAFE, I'VE BEEN THIS WAY MANY TIMES! YOU MUST TRUST ME!

4 PRAYER PAGE

King Jesus

10 Look at Jesus

Father, when I'm tempted to fight back and lash out because somebody has upset me, remind me of Jesus quietly standing there, taking the abuse, the cutting remarks, the mockery. Forgive me when I bring shame on the Name of Jesus by the way I treat other people. It's so easy to be rude and inconsiderate.

(49, page 74)

11 King of my life

So many voices shouting, so many philosophies and ideologies, different cults and groups—all powerful forces wanting to control my life, telling me they have the answer. Jesus is the King. He rules and I know there is no one else to compare with Him. Help me to crown Him the King of my life, giving Him the honour He deserves.

(50, page 76)

12 New life in Jesus

What have I got to be proud of? I doubt if I could even fill a couple of minutes adding up all that is worthwhile in my life, and yet I am so proud. Proud of this achievement, of that ability, of succeeding at .... Forgive me, and make me realize how much You have to give me—pardon, forgiveness, cleansing and new life in Jesus Christ.

(18, page 36)

UNDER FIRE!
YOUR FAITH

Challenges to your faith come from many directions. Some friends may be sceptical about what you believe. They may say: 'You've been brainwashed.' Or: 'You're just going through a religious phase. We want a lot more proof before we're going to believe. Your faith is based on emotion not truth.'

Other groups might point out that your interpretation of the faith is all wrong. 'We are right: you must accept our system,' they argue.

There's nothing new in opposition of this kind. It has existed as long as the good news about Jesus Christ has been proclaimed. John, the disciple of Jesus, had come across many attempts to unsettle Christians so he wrote words of reassurance about their faith (see *sections 56-58*).

56

Loving God and His family

If you believe that Jesus is the Christ—that he is God's Son and your Saviour—then you are a child of God. And all who love the Father love his children too.

So you can find out how much you love God's children—your brothers and sisters in the Lord—by how much you love and obey God. Loving God means doing what he tells us to do, and really that isn't hard at all; for every child of God can obey him, defeating sin and evil pleasure by trusting Christ to help him.

1 John chapter 5, verses 1-4

How do you get on with your family? Not so much the family at home, although that is also important, but rather with your new family—your Christian brothers and sisters. It won't be a perfect group, but be honest and ask yourself, 'Am I ever guilty of back-biting and complaining without cause?'

If you find it hard to get on well with other Christians, it's probably because your relationship with God is faulty. Your complaining and resentment are in fact signs of a rebellion against God. Once your relationship with Him is put right, then your other relationships will improve. As your love for God develops, so your love for others will also grow.

Think, then pray: How does my love work out in practice?

SNAP!
BACKBITING

57

Witnesses to the truth

But who could possibly fight and win this battle except by believing that Jesus is truly the Son of God?

And we know he is, because God said so with a voice from heaven when Jesus was baptized, and again as he was facing death . . . And the Holy Spirit, for ever truthful, says it too. So we have these three witnesses: the voice of the Holy Spirit in our hearts, the voice from heaven at Christ's baptism, and the voice before he died. And they all say the same thing: that Jesus Christ is the Son of God.

All who believe this know in their hearts that it is true. If anyone doesn't believe this, he is actually calling God a liar, because he doesn't believe what God has said about his Son.

1 John chapter 5, verses 5-8, 10

One way to be sure whether you are a Christian or not is to ask yourself, 'Do I listen to God and believe what He says?' Often we try to live on a second-hand type of faith. We listen to what *others* say about God and believe what *they* say. But we fail to make time or take the trouble to listen to Him.

God wants us to know the truth and today's reading mentions *three* witnesses. Who are they? And to what truth are they testifying?

Listen to God now.

58

Being sure . . . by talking to God

And what is it that God has said? That he has given us eternal life, and that this life is in his Son. So whoever has God's Son has life; whoever does not have his Son, does not have life.

I have written this to you who believe in the Son of God so that you may know you have eternal life. And we are sure of this, that he will listen to us whenever we ask him for anything in line with his will. And if we really know he is listening when we talk to him and make our requests, then we can be sure that he will answer us.

1 John chapter 5, verses 11-15

Another way to be sure that we are going the Jesus way is to ask: 'Do I talk to God in prayer?'

- *God is always open to us.* We can talk to Him at any time, but it is helpful to have a regular time for prayer—not just when we feel like it.
- *God listens to us.* He takes note of what we ask for, but we must not try to twist His arm. As we face up to what prayer is we discover what God wants for us.
- *God answers us.* Make your own prayer diary.

Write down topics to pray about regularly, then as you look back you will see how God is working.

Lord, help me not just to talk and think about prayer, but really to put it into practice.

59

Hope for the future

See how very much our heavenly Father loves us, for he allows us to be called his children . . .

Yes, dear friends, we are already God's children, right now, and we can't even imagine what it is going to be like later on. But we do know this, that when he comes we will be like him, as a result of seeing him as he really is. And everyone who really believes this will try to stay pure because Christ is pure.

1 John chapter 3, verses 1-3

People ask us about the future. But we haven't got all the answers. We do know, however, that God is in control of events, and that the climax of history will be the visible reappearance of Jesus Christ.

And then there's heaven: we don't know all the details about it, because our language can only speak in terms of this world. But we can be sure that we shall be with God and see Him.

If we have these certain hopes for the *future*, they should affect the *present*. We must resist temptation with the help of Jesus Christ. We must concentrate on removing from our lives whatever hinders our Christian development.

Lord, I want my confidence for the future to be real, based on what You are going to do. Help me not to think so much about tomorrow that I forget to follow You today.

60

Stay close

Those who keep on sinning are against God, for every sin is done against the will of God. And you know that he became a man so that he could take away our sins, and that there is no sin in him, no missing of God's will at any time in any way. So if we stay close to him, obedient to him, we won't be sinning either; but as for those who keep on sinning, they should realize this: they sin because they have never really known him or become his.

The person who has been born into God's family does not make a practice of sinning, because now God's life is in him; so he can't keep on sinning, for this new life has been born into him and controls him—he has been born again.

1 John chapter 3, verses 4-6, 9

It's all too easy to become a 'second-rate' Christian because contact with Christ the Leader has been lost. Fix your attention on Him rather than on yourself and your problems.

Use this check list regularly. Do I . . .

Spend time alone in Jesus' company, thinking about His words?

Share regularly with others what God has done for me?

Apply to myself all God's standards—those that are demanding as well as the easier ones?

Immediately come to God asking for His forgiveness and strength when I am disobedient or am tempted to do wrong?

Talk to Him now.

61
Love in action

So now we can tell who is a child of God and who belongs to Satan. Whoever is living a life of sin and doesn't love his brother shows that he is not in God's family; for the message to us from the beginning has been that we should love one another.

We know what real love is from Christ's example in dying for us. And so we also ought to lay down our lives for our Christian brothers.

But if someone who is supposed to be a Christian has money enough to live well, and sees a brother in need, and won't help him—how can God's love be within him? Little children, let us stop just saying we love people; let us really love them, and show it by our actions.

1 John chapter 3, verses 10, 11, 16-18

Have you ever found yourself listening to someone but at the same time planning what you are going to do next? Giving your whole attention to people, and not just concentrating on getting your own ideas across, is putting love into action. But it's more than that. Are you prepared to give yourself and your money (*see 36*) to help others without expecting *anything* in return?

Are you as eager to befriend the 'awkward' person as you are the easy-going and popular person? Ask God to help you to give all your attention to the people you meet today.

62

Loving the Jesus way

God showed how much he loved us by sending his only Son into this wicked world to bring to us eternal life through his death. In this act we see what real love is: it is not our love for God, but his love for us when he sent his Son to satisfy God's anger against our sins.

Dear friends, since God loved us as much as that, we surely ought to love each other too. For though we have never yet seen God, when we love each other God lives in us and his love within us grows ever stronger. And he has put his own Holy Spirit into our hearts as a proof to us that we are living with him and he with us. And furthermore, we have seen with our own eyes and now tell all the world that God sent his Son to be their Saviour.

1 John chapter 4, verses 9-14

'I don't want to get involved. I'll give some money but don't ask me to go and help.'

God's love challenges our selfishness because Jesus is involved in the lives of men and women, exposing Himself to rejection and hostility.

'He does such stupid things,' we may say as we write off a friend as 'impossible'. But Jesus tackles our problems, and understanding people is where we must begin—however difficult they may be.

If God's love has created a new life for *you*, ask Him to help *you* to show His love to others.

LOVING AND LIVING

Love is

•God sending Jesus to save me.
•God reaching out towards me, wanting to pick me up.
•God surrounding me with the warmth of His affection.

Love means

•accepting all that God offers.
•depending on God as His child.
•sharing with Him both my joys and sorrows.

Love grows

•as I allow God to help me.
•as I face the challenge of helping others.
•as I see the greatness of the love of Jesus.

Love develops

•as my love for others becomes more important than my love for self.
•as my privileges as God's child are realized and experienced.

Love produces

- life that is pure and good, devoted to God's service.
- resistance to destructive forces.
- thankfulness to God for all His blessings.

Father, I know that Your love is constantly available to me. Forgive all my hardness and bitterness. I want my love for You and others to grow and to produce praise to Your holy Name.

63

I know because . . .

We know how much God loves us because we have felt his love and because we believe him when he tells us that he loves us dearly. God is love, and anyone who lives in love is living with God and God is living in him. And as we live with Christ, our love grows more perfect and complete; so we will not be ashamed and embarrassed t the day of judgement, but can face him with confidence and joy, because he loves us and we love him too.

1 John chapter 4, verses 16, 17

'How can I be sure about God's love? There are two parts to the answer in the Bible reading.

Firstly—personal experience. Can you recall certain occasions when you have been specially aware of God's love? You may have been puzzled—and He directed you. Anxious—and He reassured you.

Secondly—God's character. He has promised to love you, and you can rely on His word. By taking God t His word, you will discover the depths of His love, not only on certain occasions but throughout every day of your life.

Share your experiences of God's love with your friends. As they hear what God has done for you, they may seek Him for themselves.

Consider what God the Father has done for you, then thank Him in word and action.

Refugee Christians

Persecution and threats of imprisonment drove the early Christians to many different areas. As a result the good news about Jesus Christ reached new areas.

Peter knew his fellow Christians would feel lonely living in strange places and settling into a different way of life. Because they were facing opposition and a new wave of persecution he sent them a letter of encouragement.

You can imagine the letter being carried by a messenger on a round trip—starting and ending at the Black Sea—travelling through Pontus, Galatia, Cappadocia, Asia and back through Bithynia. This area is modern Turkey.

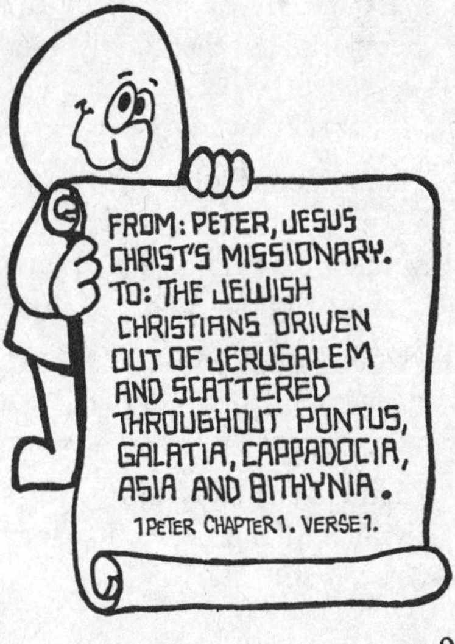

64

Enjoying family life

Dear friends, God the Father chose you long ago and knew you would become his children. And the Holy Spirit has been at work in your hearts, cleansing you with the blood of Jesus Christ and enabling you to please him. May God bless you richly and grant you increasing freedom from all anxiety and fear.

All honour to God, the God and Father of our Lord Jesus Christ; for it is his boundless mercy that has given us the privilege of being born again, so that we are now members of God's own family.

1 Peter chapter 1, verses 2, 3

How much do you value the various families of which you are a member? You belong to the family in which you have grown up, and the family you may have joined by marriage. If you are going the Jesus way, then you are a member of another family—the family of God.

Thank You, Father, because You have adopted me into Your family. I know I can approach You at any time. Make me aware of my responsibilities to You and others who love You as I do.

Thank You, Lord, that through Your death I receive forgiveness for sins, and that Your resurrection gives me confidence for the future.

Thank You, Holy Spirit, for showing me myself and for giving me the power to live for Jesus.

65

Reserved for you

God has reserved for his children the priceless gift of eternal life; it is kept in heaven for you, pure and undefiled, beyond the reach of change and decay. And God, in his mighty power, will make sure that you get there safely to receive it, because you are trusting him. It will be yours in that coming last day for all to see. So be truly glad! There is wonderful joy ahead, even though the going is rough for a while down here.

These trials are only to test your faith ... It is being tested as fire tests gold and purifies it—and your faith is far more precious to God than mere gold. So if your faith remains strong after being tried in the test tube of fiery trials, it will bring you much praise and glory and honour on the day of his return.

1 Peter chapter 1, verses 4-7

• *What is heaven?* Heaven is where God is, and God's children can look forward to going there. It is full of reserved places waiting for their rightful occupants.

• *Who goes there?* Only those who trust in Christ as Saviour *now* can be sure of their places. Those who reject Him find themselves in another reserved place—hell.

God is in control—both in heaven and in this life. If you are going through a tough time, remember that all God's resources are available to help you now. Use prayer [15] on page 104.

66

Don't slip back

Obey God because you are his children; don't slip back into your old ways—doing evil because you knew no better. But be holy now in everything you do, just as the Lord is holy . . .

And remember that your heavenly Father to whom you pray has no favourites when he judges. He will judge you with perfect justice for everything you do; so act in reverent fear of him from now on until you get to heaven.

1 Peter chapter 1, verses 14, 15, 17

'Why should I work harder than everybody else when nobody ever thanks me?'

The constant influence of those around us makes it easy to slide back. Here are some safeguards against becoming slack.

•My mind must be informed. A serious study of God's Word will help me to answer questions about the faith. As my understanding of God's ways grows, so will my confidence in Him.

•I must remember that God's standards are absolute. If I measure my conduct by what others say and do, then I'll soon be in trouble. There is constant temptation to compromise, whereas God demands complete holiness.

Ask God to help you to be honest with yourself. Then confess to Him the ways in which you've lowered your standards.

LUST
LIES
SELFISHNESS
ENVY
HATE

67

What money can't buy

God paid a ransom to save you from the impossible road to heaven which your fathers tried to take, and the ransom he paid was not mere gold or silver, as you very well know; but he paid for you with the precious lifeblood of Christ, the sinless, spotless Lamb of God.

God chose him for this purpose long before the world began, but only recently was he brought into public view, in these last days, as a blessing to you. Because of this your trust can be in God who raised Christ from the dead and gave him great glory. Now your faith and hope can rest in him alone.

1 Peter chapter 1, verses 18-21

Have you ever stopped to think about the various reasons people give as to why *they* should go to heaven? 'I'm a law-abiding citizen and I've never harmed anybody.' 'I always give to charity, and occasionally to the church.' And so on . . . But they cannot talk or buy their way to heaven. Jesus Christ has opened up the way.

- He died on the cross to pay the price for our sins—do *you* believe this?
- His resurrection assures us that death is not the end, and that there's a place in heaven for those who follow Him *now*.

Think about the 'price' God paid for you, then talk to Him in prayer.

HOW MUCH FOR A LITTLE OL' ROOM IN HEAVEN?... WHATEVER IT COSTS• I'LL DOUBLE IT! WHY I'LL EVEN...

5 PRAYER PAGE

Pointing people to Jesus

13 Getting involved with people

I remember how Jesus' love always moved Him to action, and I pray that I may be more concerned for others than myself. Stop me from holding back, even when it is costly to love and when I realize the sacrifice required of me.
(76, page 117)

14 Growing in faith

Thank You, Father, for giving me faith in Jesus, and for the assurance that I belong to Him. Help me to put my faith into practice so that my confidence in Jesus grows.
(76, page 117)

15 Looking ahead

If I become bothered and depressed, Lord, please remind me of the great adventure in store for me when I get to heaven. It's good to have this hope in the future, but I pray that it won't become an escape from my responsibilities in this life.
(65, page 99)

PRAY DAILY

68

What you can rely on

You have a new life. It was not passed on to you from your parents, for the life they gave you will fade away. This new one will last forever, for it comes from Christ, God's ever-living message to men.

Yes, our natural lives will fade as grass does when it becomes all brown and dry. All our greatness is like a flower that droops and falls; but the Word of the Lord will last for ever.

1 Peter chapter 1, verses 23-25

'It won't last,' declares the cynic pouring cold water on the enthusiasm of a new Christian. 'What about your other bright ideas that have faded away?' Such words may well cause secret doubts in the mind of the person accused. But Peter reminds us that Christians have been given gifts that no one can take away from them.

•*Life that lasts for ever.* A Christian is a person who has been reborn. Jesus Christ has taken up residence in the life of the child of God and He will never abandon His followers.

•*Christ the living Word.* He is the same in every age—He doesn't change. Whatever people may say about Him, He is always available to us.

•*The Bible.* In spite of much critical examination it stands as the uniquely inspired account of God's dealings with His people. And it is through the knowledge of God's Word that we grow in Him.

69
Growing strong

Get rid of your feelings of hatred. Don't just pretend to be good! Be done with dishonesty and jealousy and talking about others behind their backs.

If you have tasted the Lord's goodness and kindness, cry for more, as a baby cries for milk—and grow strong in the Lord. Come to Christ, who is the living Foundation of Rock upon which God builds; though men have spurned him, he is very precious to God who has chosen him above all others.

1 Peter chapter 2, verses 1-4

'I hate him because of what he's done to me.' Although these words are often said in a moment of anger, they reflect a deep feeling of hurt.

'I'm right, and he is wrong'—words that can be repeated until you have convinced yourself; but you are the poorer for such an attitude. An unwillingness to forgive is a sign of self-love. Such a destructive process must be halted.

- Say sorry to Jesus Christ—and to the person you hate, if that will help.
- Claim Christ's forgiveness and, if possible, the pardon of the person you've offended.
- Ask for God's help to love that person, then look for occasions to be kind.

Father, help me to search my heart and to discover whether I am hating anyone.

70

Ingredients for worship

Now you have become ... his holy priests; so come to him (you are acceptable to him because of Jesus Christ) and offer to God those things that please him.

... You have been chosen by God himself—you are priests of the King, you are holy and pure, you are God's very own—all this so that you may show to others how God called you out of the darkness into his wonderful light. Once you were less than nothing; now you are God's own. Once you knew very little of God's kindness; now your very lives have been changed by it.

1 Peter chapter 2, verses 5, 9, 10

Each Christian is a priest—and a priest's job is to worship God. What is the recipe for worship?

Take several hymns, add a few prayers, mix in some Bible readings and a sermon ... If that is all that makes up our worship, it will never 'rise'. We need something extra: thanksgiving—gratitude to God for the change He's made in our lives; repentance—when we become more aware of our own inabilities and failings than of our good points, God will listen to us; a genuine concern for others —learning to work with others is hard, and we must be tolerant.

Remember, the quality of our fellowship often makes or mars our worship.

Prayer [7] on page 75 is for today.

71
Operation Andrew

You are only visitors here. Since your real home is in heaven I beg you to keep away from the evil pleasures of this world; they are not for you, for they fight against your very souls.

Be careful how you behave among your unbelieving neighbours; for then, even if they are suspicious of you and talk against you, they will end up praising God for your good works when Christ returns.

1 Peter chapter 2, verses 11, 12

Peter was well aware of the importance of relationships. He had been introduced to Jesus by his brother Andrew, and such personal introductions continue to be one of the most effective ways of spreading the good news. But the timing is always vital.

- Have I made an effort to get to know and understand the people next door?
- Have I prayed for an opportunity to share my faith with them?
- Am I learning to talk naturally about Jesus without becoming tense?
- Is my life consistent enough to commend Jesus to other people?

You know my neighbours and friends, Lord—help me to be sensitive to their needs. I know there are things that I say and do that probably annoy them and are dishonouring to You. Please give me the desire to put this right.

I MUST TELL FRED THAT I'M NOW...
BIBLE
...TOO LATE!

72

Freedom from—what?

It is God's will that your good lives should silence those who foolishly condemn the Gospel without knowing what it can do for them, having never experienced its power . . . Live as those who are free to do only God's will at all times.

Show respect for everyone. Love Christians everywhere. Fear God and honour the government.

Servants, you must respect your masters and do whatever they tell you—not only if they are kind and reasonable, but even if they are tough and cruel.

1 Peter chapter 2, verses 15-18

Freedom fighters . . . civil liberties . . . human rights. These words reflect the powerful desire for freedom from various kinds of oppression. If you are going the Jesus way, then you have an inner freedom: you have been set free from the compulsion to do wrong. This will lead you to a desire to help people instead of merely being obsessed with your own needs and interests.

The freedom Christ gives you brings great responsibilities. You must be ready to challenge accepted ideas, including the popular cry for my '*rights*' whenever it is opposed to my '*responsibilities*'. True freedom knows how to accept hardships.

Lord, as I rejoice in the freedom You give, please set me free to serve others.

73

In the footsteps of Jesus

Praise the Lord if you are punished for doing right!

This suffering is all part of the work God has given you. Christ, who suffered for you, is your example. Follow in his steps: he never sinned, never told a lie, never answered back when insulted; when he suffered he did not threaten to get even; he left his case in the hands of God who always judges fairly. He personally carried the load of our sins in his own body when he died on the cross, so that we can be finished with sin and live a good life from now on. For his wounds have healed ours! Like sheep you wandered away from God, but now you have returned to your Shepherd, the Guardian of your souls who keeps you safe from all attacks.

1 Peter chapter 2, verses 19, 21-25

Do you ever find yourself thinking . . . ? 'It was easier for Jesus, He was different.' If you do, then remember that He was tempted just as we are because He was a man. And because He was the Son of God, He also had to face temptation at that level. Or you may think, 'Times and situations have changed.' But, remember, people nd their basic needs are still the same.

If you follow in Christ's steps today, what difference should it make?

Thank God for the patient endurance of Jesus Christ when He suffered.

74
Friction in the home

Wives, fit in with your husbands' plans; for then if they refuse to listen when you talk to them about the Lord, they will be won by your respectful, pure behaviour. Your godly lives will speak to them better than any words.

Don't be concerned about the outward beauty that depends on jewellery, or beautiful clothes, or hair arrangement. Be beautiful inside, in your hearts, with the lasting charm of a gentle and quiet spirit which is so precious to God.

You husbands must be careful of your wives, being thoughtful of their needs and honouring them as the weaker sex. Remember that you and your wife are partners in receiving God's blessings, and if you don't treat her as you should, your prayers will not get ready answers.

1 Peter chapter 3, verses 1-4, 7

If we are going to love the Jesus way at home, we should avoid friction and show consideration for the needs of others.

A couple's faith develops as they learn to be honest and frank with each other, and are open to God in shared prayer. Think about the words, 'partners in receiving God's blessings'.

But there's a word here, too, for single people as well: beauty is only skin deep—it's what we're like inside that matters to God.

Thank God for the open Christian homes through which you have been helped.

IT'S ALL YOUR FAULT!

Non-friction—what the family means

Jesus' followers belong to a new family. Each person has something to contribute and to receive from the Christian community. The help of friends when we are in trouble, someone to laugh with us—these are part of the Christian adventure of sharing together. In these ways we discover what sort of people we are—our rough edges begin to be smoothed off. We learn about God as we depend on Him. Through friendship with one another we appreciate the needs and problems of others.

HI, BROTHER!

75

I wish . . .

And now this word to all of you: You should be like one big happy family, full of sympathy towards each other, loving one another with tender hearts and humble minds. Don't repay evil for evil. Don't snap back at those who say unkind things about you. Instead, pray for God's help for them, for we are to be kind to others, and God will bless us for it.

If you want a happy, good life, keep control of your tongue, and guard your lips from telling lies. Turn away from evil and do good. Try to live in peace even if you must run after it to catch and hold it. For the Lord is watching his children, listening to their prayers; but the Lord's face is hard against those who do evil.

1 Peter chapter 3, verses 8-12

It's often said, 'If only I'd thought first and *then* spoken, things might have been so different. Who would have thought that those few words could cause so much harm?'

If you can't say anything good about a person, don't say anything at all. Even if we start by saying, 'I'd like you to pray for so and so because . . .' we can be guilty of gossiping.

Check point • Is all my conversation clean and helpful?

Lord, please forgive my thoughtless and cruel words. Give me control over my tongue.

76

Christian standards

Usually no one will hurt you for wanting to do good. But even if they should, you are to be envied, for God will reward you for it. Quietly trust yourself to Christ your Lord and if anybody asks why you believe as you do, be ready to tell him, and do it in a gentle and respectful way.

Do what is right; then if men speak against you, calling you evil names, they will become ashamed of themselves for falsely accusing you when you have only done what is good. Remember, if God wants you to suffer, it is better to suffer for doing good than for doing wrong.

Christ also suffered. He died once for the sins of all us guilty sinners, although he himself was innocent of any sin at any time, that he might bring us safely home to God.

1 Peter chapter 3, verses 13-18

'I don't know why you bother helping him—he's not worth it,' exclaims your friend. But if you are going to love the Jesus way, then you must treat everyone fairly and equally in spite of misunderstandings.

'You're mad, you ought to "adjust" your expense account the same as everyone else does.' The people you work with may laugh at your honesty, but, privately, wish they had your courage. Your quiet protest is often an effective Christian witness.

Prayers [13] and [14] on page 104 are for today.

77

Dealing with suffering

Since Christ suffered and underwent pain, you must have the same attitude he had; you must be ready to suffer, too. For remember, when your body suffers, sin loses its power, and you won't be spending the rest of your life chasing after evil desires, but will be anxious to do the will of God. You have had enough in the past of the evil things the godless enjoy—sexual sin, lust, getting drunk, wild parties, drinking bouts, and the worship of idols—which leads to other terrible sins.

Of course, your former friends will be very surprised when you don't eagerly join them any more in the wicked things they do, and they will laugh at you in contempt and scorn. But just remember that they must face the Judge of all, living and dead; they will be punished for the way they have lived.

1 Peter chapter 4, verses 1-5

Sometimes you feel up against it—there's pressure on your particular weak spot or anxiety about relationships. What resources have you to tackle the problem?

Friends may say: 'Forget about it, escape from it.' But suffering of any kind either brings you nearer to God or drives you further away from Him. How you deal with it matters. You can build a barrier of resentment, or open the way to a stronger dependence on God.

You might like to use prayer [9] on page 75 which is for today.

78

Full steam ahead

The end of the world is coming soon. Therefore be earnest, thoughtful men of prayer. Most important of all, continue to show deep love for each other, for love makes up for many of your faults. Cheerfully share your home with those who need a meal or a place to stay for the night.

God has given each of you some special abilities; be sure to use them to help each other, passing on to others God's many kinds of blessings. Are you called to preach? Then preach as though God himself were speaking through you. Are you called to help others? Do it with all the strength and energy that God supplies, so that God will be glorified through Jesus Christ . . .

1 Peter chapter 4, verses 7-11

'Being in the right place at the right time, doing the right thing—sounds marvellous, but how can I be sure that God has called me to this particular task?' This question has troubled many thoughtful Christians.

God's call can come in different ways. Another Christian sees a potential in you that you don't recognize. He asks, 'Have you ever considered . . . ?' If it is God's call, an inner assurance will grow and develop, but Peter reminds us that we are to be thoughtful men and women of prayer.

Ask God to bring out your hidden abilities and to equip you for His work.

79
On trial

Dear friends, don't be bewildered or surprised when you go through the fiery trials ahead . . . Instead, be really glad —because these trials will make you partners with Christ in his suffering, and afterwards you will have the wonderful joy of sharing his glory in that coming day when it will be displayed.

Be happy if you are cursed and insulted for being a Christian, for when that happens the Spirit of God will come upon you with great glory. Don't let me hear of your suffering for murdering or stealing or making trouble or being a busybody and prying into other people's affairs. But it is no shame to suffer for being a Christian. Praise God for the privilege of being in Christ's family and being called by his wonderful name!

1 Peter chapter 4, verses 12-16

When you are criticized because you're going the Jesus way, don't answer back. Silently thank God that it's been realized that you are a Christian. If there's a joke at your expense, don't scowl and become tense, smile and ask God to help you to remain calm. Such people are not at all sure of themselves. They are trying you to see if you have any extra strength.

Share these situations with others. Together, praise God for the support and encouragement He gives. Use prayer [18] on page 122.

HA! HA! HA!
HE! HE! HE!

6 PRAYER PAGE

God in control

16 Prayer for guidance

Forgive me when I try to manage on my own. I know that You can give answers to my problems and show me the way to live. When I'm puzzled help me to pray quickly, 'What do You want me to do?'
(54, page 81)

17 When the pressure is on . . .

Lord, when the pressure is on I know that I need to turn to You instead of running away from difficulties. Help me to bear the ridicule of my friends, and to take every opportunity of sharing my faith with them.
(27, page 46)

18 Praising God

It's too easy to grumble. Instead, let me see that in every situation, however tough it may be, there is something for which I can praise and thank You.
(79, page 120)

PRAY DAILY

80

Stand firm

Let God have all your worries and cares, for he is always thinking about you and watching everything that concerns you.

Be careful—watch out for attacks from Satan, your great enemy. He prowls around like a hungry, roaring lion, looking for some victim to tear apart. Stand firm when he attacks. Trust the Lord . . .

After you have suffered a little while, our God, who is full of kindness through Christ, will give you his eternal glory. He personally will come and pick you up, and set you firmly in place, and make you stronger than ever. To him be all power over all things, for ever and ever. Amen.

1 Peter chapter 5, verses 7-11

Satan is a master of disguises. He can be openly and aggressively evil, or he may cunningly appear as goodness itself. Lies and deceit are his trade mark. He wants you to think that he is all powerful and that it is useless to resist evil. But his power is broken. Jesus, by His death on the cross and resurrection, defeated him and conquered the forces of evil.

Resist Satan by fixing your eyes on Jesus and asking for His help. Deliberately turn away from all evil thoughts and actions, and stand firm in the strength God is willing to give.

Prayer [6] on page 45 is for today.

Followers of . . .

We live in times of change and upheaval. The world is insistent, urging us to follow its pattern. But we must avoid being moulded by materialism and self-worship and instead challenge the world with our Christian lifestyle.

When Christ is central to all we say and do, our friends, work-mates and neighbours will sit up and take notice that we are followers of JESUS.

Loving the Jesus way

Guide to contents

Scripture Union
LIVING TRUTH SERIES
LOVING THE JESUS WAY
LIVING THE JESUS WAY
GROWING THE JESUS WAY
GOING THE JESUS WAY
MAKE SURE YOU GET ALL FOUR!
4 BOOKS FOR THOSE WHO WANT TO COME TO GRIPS WITH THE TEACHING OF THE NEW TESTAMENT.
AVAILABLE FROM ALL CHRISTIAN BOOKSHOPS